Riding the Settle & Carlisle
1969–1989

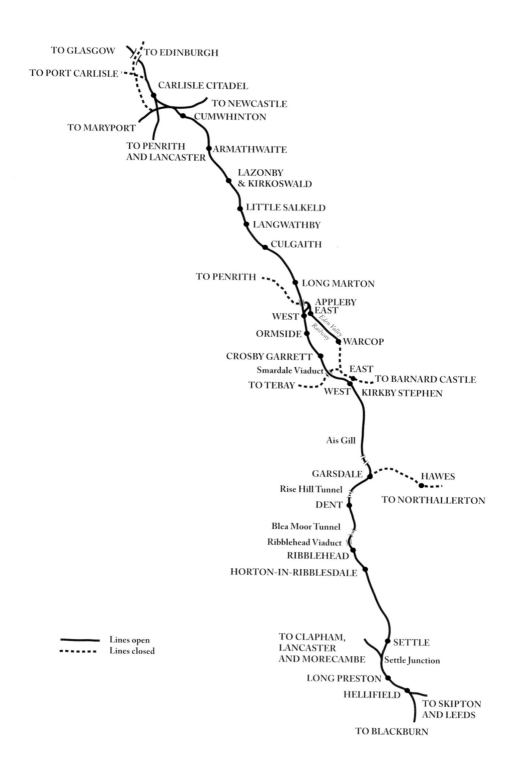

TO GLASGOW
TO EDINBURGH
TO PORT CARLISLE
CARLISLE CITADEL
TO NEWCASTLE
CUMWHINTON
TO MARYPORT
TO PENRITH
AND LANCASTER
ARMATHWAITE
LAZONBY
& KIRKOSWALD
LITTLE SALKELD
LANGWATHBY
CULGAITH
TO PENRITH
LONG MARTON
APPLEBY
EAST
WEST
Eden Valley Railway
ORMSIDE
WARCOP
CROSBY GARRETT
EAST
Smardale Viaduct
TO BARNARD CASTLE
TO TEBAY
WEST
KIRKBY STEPHEN
Ais Gill
GARSDALE
HAWES
Rise Hill Tunnel
DENT
TO NORTHALLERTON
Blea Moor Tunnel
Ribblehead Viaduct
RIBBLEHEAD
HORTON-IN-RIBBLESDALE
TO CLAPHAM,
LANCASTER
AND MORECAMBE
SETTLE
Settle Junction
LONG PRESTON
HELLIFIELD
TO SKIPTON
AND LEEDS
TO BLACKBURN

Lines open
Lines closed

RIDING THE SETTLE & CARLISLE

1969-1989

A Companion and Guide

David Mather

Silver Link Publishing Ltd

For my wife Mair, in thanks
for her continued support and encouragement

First published in 2011

British Library Cataloguing in Publication Data

A catalogue record for this book is available from
the British Library.

ISBN 978 1 85794 384 9

Silver Link Publishing Ltd
The Trundle
Ringstead Road
Great Addington
Kettering
Northants NN14 4BW

Tel/Fax: 01536 330588
email: sales@nostalgiacollection.com
Website: www.nostalgiacollection.com

Printed and bound in the Czech Republic

All photographs were taken by the author.

Preface

This volume is your companion as you ride the Long Drag. It is also my story of the mighty Settle & Carlisle Railway, from the difficult days following the demise of steam, through the agony of proposed closure and into the dawn of the preservation era.

So buy your ticket, climb aboard, sit back, let the story unfold and soak up the legend that is the Settle & Carlisle Railway.

Riding the Settle & Carlisle

Typical Gradients

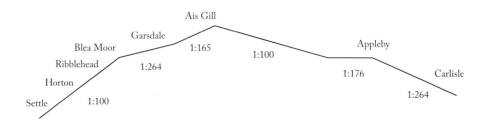

The gradient profile indicating the main features of the line.

Preserved Stanier 'Pacific' No 46229 *Duchess of Hamilton* reaches Ais Gill summit with the southbound 'Cumbrian Mountain Pullman' in November 1983.

Contents

Looking towards the south end of Blea Moor Tunnel, with Blea Moor's Home signal in the foreground.

1
The 'Railway King' and the birth of the Midland Railway

In the 1830s several companies were formed for the purpose of building railways in the Midlands. These included the Midland Counties (Nottingham to Derby), the North Midland (Derby to Leeds), the York & North Midland (York to Newcastle-upon-Tyne), and the Birmingham & Derby. In 1844 George Hudson masterminded the amalgamation of these small companies to form the Midland Railway Company.

Born at Howsham between York and Malton in 1800, George Hudson moved to York at the age of 15. In 1827, upon the death of his great-uncle, a wealthy gentleman farmer named Matthew Bottrill, he inherited a considerable fortune, which changed his life. He bought a mansion in Monkgate, York, which still carries a plaque in his honour.

He invested heavily in railways, notably the North Midland and the York & North Midland, and in this he was ably assisted by the talented architect George Townsend Andrews. Andrews designed not only the stations, but all the buildings for the York & North Midland Railway from 1839 onwards. In particular, he was responsible for the design for a new station at York commissioned jointly by the Y&NM and the Great North of England Railway and opened in 1841. His architect practice in York was not limited solely to the design of railway buildings, but was responsible for a number of churches and the headquarters of two York-based banks. He became Sheriff of York in 1846-47 during George Hudson's third term as Mayor. Andrews died in 1855 at the age of 51 and is buried in York Cemetery. His grave, in an overgrown section of this vast burial ground of more than 120,000 graves, is easily overlooked, and even when located is not impressive for a man whose influence had been so far-reaching during his lifetime and whose legacy lives on so long after his death.

By the mid-1840s Hudson was at his most powerful, working for a while with

The entrance to George Hudson House, 44 Monkgate, York.

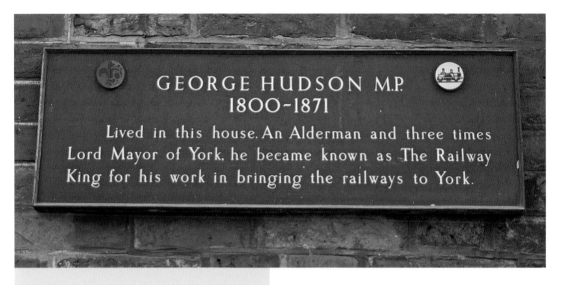

GEORGE HUDSON M.P.
1800-1871

Lived in this house. An Alderman and three times
Lord Mayor of York, he became known as The Railway
King for his work in bringing the railways to York.

The plaque on the wall of the house, commemorating his residence.

George Stephenson and benefiting from the support of the then Prime Minister, the Duke of Wellington. He built the York to Scarborough railway line and of course ensured that it went via Howsham! His line from York to Leeds via Tadcaster, however, was never completed, though the impressive viaduct over the River Wharfe in Tadcaster still stands today.

Hudson enlarged the enterprise of which he was Chairman and leading shareholder by adding the Birmingham & Gloucester and Bristol & Gloucester companies in 1845, giving him control of more than 1,000 miles of line. Ultimately the company would grow to have lines from its origins in the Derby area to London, Manchester, Liverpool, Bristol, South Wales, Bournemouth, Yarmouth, Lancaster and, of course, Carlisle. In addition, in Scotland, its partners the North British Railway and Glasgow & South Western Railway took its trains on to Glasgow, Edinburgh and Aberdeen. At his peak the 'Railway King' controlled 33% of the entire British railway system.

However, by the late 1840s falling share prices as the Railway Mania bubble burst, and investigations into Hudson's dubious business

The final resting place of George Townsend Andrews (1804-55) in York Cemetery. His name is engraved on the far side, obscured from view by the overgrown vegetation.

The crest of the Midland Railway company incorporates the arms of the principal towns served by the railway, including Birmingham, Bristol, Derby, Leeds, Leicester and Lincoln.

dealings, carried out to a significant degree by his political and business opponent George Leeman, brought about his downfall. Exposing as they did outrageous frauds, numerous illegal share dealings and the discovery of his bribery of MPs, he was left ruined. Leeman went on to be a successful businessman and Member of Parliament for York, while Hudson was incarcerated in York Castle in 1865 as a debtor. Eventually friends raised money to release him, whereupon he disappeared into retirement in London until his death at the age of 68. Nevertheless, his creation, the Midland Railway, grew from strength to strength. Inspired leadership and dogged determination would be essential if this young company was to continue to prosper during the turbulent years ahead, and bring to fruition the vision that would become the Settle & Carlisle Railway.

2
The line that should never have been built?

Construction of the Settle & Carlisle Railway between 1869 and 1876 was a massive undertaking through England's most inhospitable landscape, involving the gouging out of 14 tunnels and the construction of no fewer than 22 viaducts. At its peak, 6,000 men laboured for an average of 10 shillings per day – very high wages for the time, equivalent to about £300 per day in 2010 (source: www.measuringworth.com). It would be the last major work carried out in the traditional 'navvy' manner, that is by men wielding picks and shovels, with transport provided by horses and tip-trucks. So that prompts the question, why invest such large sums of money in building a railway here?

The line takes the middle course to the North, the only possible one that nature had left between the two existing routes. It was the product of inter-company rivalry together with over-inflated egos, and would not have been constructed at all if the London & North Western Railway and Midland Railway had been able to reach a sensible arrangement about the use of the Lancaster & Carlisle system.

The S&C's conception came late in the railway building age. By the time Sharland, the Midland Railway's engineer, had spent ten days walking the entire course of the line and making his survey, several of the great railway pioneers were already dead, notably George Hudson, Joseph Locke, I. K. Brunel, George Stephenson, and even his famous son, Robert. Sharland's instructions were clear – to build a direct route whatever the cost. There was no question of 'swinging into hillsides', horseshoe-like, if a valley was to be crossed. Similarly, if rocky moorland lay in the path of the railway, there was only one course to be taken – blast straight through it.

The country beyond Settle is awesome. The high peaks and rugged dales are challenging at the best of times but, with weather that can become wild without warning, the route engineers and their hordes of navvies had been set a Herculean task, battling constantly against bog and boulder clay. Add to this 73 miles at a ruling gradient of 1 in 100 and the enormity of the challenge unfolds. The cost of building the line was £3.5 million (more than £2 billion today), about 20 times the cost of building a comparable length of track anywhere else in England at the time. It was over this route that the Midland Railway set out to pioneer a standard of passenger comfort and service that would be without equal amongst the railway companies of the time, relying as it did on that 'inspired leadership and dogged determination' mentioned earlier.

The end of the line?

Steam haulage on our nation's railways ended during 1968, amid great sadness in enthusiasts' eyes. At that time most of us believed that we had witnessed the end of steam. The preservation movement was little more than a dream. To make matters worse, a move was afoot to close this masterpiece of Victorian endeavour, this testament to the visionaries of the railway age. The Settle & Carlisle line was cited as being grossly uneconomical – too expensive to maintain, tunnels leaking, viaducts decaying, trackbeds

crumbling, station buildings falling into disrepair. Surely it must be closed?

The 'British Railways Passenger Services Timetable for Trains from London, The Midlands, North Wales and the North' for the period from 17 June to 8 September 1963 makes interesting reading when comparing provision with that of later years. Table 218 lists a total of 17 'weekday' services between Leeds and Carlisle, though a third of these are 'Saturdays Excepted' (SX) or 'Saturdays Only' (SO), and one, the first train of the day from Leeds, is 'Mondays Excepted' (2.00am) or 'Mondays Only' (2.06am). Several of the services are London St Pancras to Glasgow St Enoch expresses and run either non-stop over the Settle & Carlisle section, or stop only at Appleby. The prestigious 'Thames-Clyde Express' restaurant car service, the 2.33pm (SX) or 2.38pm (SO) from Leeds, was the most notable amongst these, stopping at Appleby only on Sundays. The line's other 'named train', the weekdays-only 1.33pm from Leeds (9.15am from St Pancras), 'The Waverley' restaurant car service to Edinburgh Waverley, made stops at Settle and Appleby. A similar timetable operated in the reverse direction, while Sunday services were limited to three or four trains in each direction, including the 'Thames-Clyde'.

The line's prestige 10.15am service from London St Pancras to Glasgow, 'The Thames-Clyde Express', had carried its name for more than 50 years before losing the title in 1975. Through London-Glasgow services continued for only two more years before being cut back to Nottingham with the commencement of the 1977/78 timetable, and from May 1982 services over the line were cut back still further; trains worked only between Leeds and Carlisle, with just two trains per day each way on Monday to Saturday and no Sunday service at all! The line was being run down.

Could anything be done to restore faith in this wonderful route?

On 24 January 1976 the official celebration of the centenary of the Settle & Carlisle line took place, and the village of Ingleton got in on the act by hosting a public meeting featuring a lecture by the celebrated

In 1975, in anticipation of the S&C's 100th birthday, the National Railway Museum in York staged its first special exhibition, 'Wheels in the Wilderness'. This centenary celebration of photographs, posters and artefacts from the Settle & Carlisle Railway attracted many admiring visitors. Officially opened on 31 March by the Bishop of Wakefield, the Right Reverend Eric Treacy, the noted railway enthusiast and photographer, it included this MR water fountain from Garsdale station, dated 1873, and this poster of the MR advertising a 'Direct Route between Principal Towns of Great Britain and North of Ireland'.

Eric Treacy commented that 'Of all the bits of railway in England, this bit, certainly to me, is the best.' He went on to describe in affectionate terms what he called 'the most exciting line in England', and finished by commenting, 'We can only hope and pray that come the end of the century it is still there.'

railway historian and engineer O. S. Nock. Arguably the greatest authority on railways of his day, he was certainly one of the most prolific, publishing more than 400 books and nearly 1,000 articles for specialist publications such as *The Railway Magazine* and *The Engineer*.

His talk stoked my enthusiasm for this project. Reflecting on the history of the line and the achievements of those who had made it possible, he went on to emphasise the crucial importance of the route both locally and nationally, stressing the need for vigilance on the part of the public at large to counter proposals being considered to downgrade or even close the line in those times of economic stringency.

Later the same year, on 1 May, Dales Rail linked its services from Carlisle with the centenary celebrations organised by British Rail and the Settle Civic Society in conjunction with the National Railway Museum, York, and Steamtown, Carnforth. Attractions included exhibitions in Settle, a station display at Carlisle and decorated stations at Settle, Ribblehead and Appleby. In addition, two special steam trains were to run between Carnforth and Carlisle and return, via Hellifield, hauled by Midland Compound No 1000 and LMS Class 5 No 44871, followed by a Grand Centenary Banquet at Settle with prizes for the best period costumes.

Dales Rail had been formed in 1975 as an experimental project to partially restore local passenger services on the line and to reopen stations to passengers during the spring

Following the talk and questions, O. S. Nock was kind enough to sign my copy of *Settle-Carlisle Railway: A Centenary Edition* by Mitchell and Joy, purchased at the Village Hall book stall at the time.

to autumn period. Its success depended on close cooperation between the Yorkshire Dales National Park, British Rail, the National Bus Company, Cumbria County Council and Eden District Council to provide increased access for visitors and restore a service for the local community by linking train and bus services in the National Park. Initially, improvements were carried out to repair and reopen the stations at Horton-in-Ribblesdale, Ribblehead, Dent, Garsdale and Kirkby Stephen to allow their use on an occasional basis after having been closed for almost five years. A fare structure designed to encourage visitors to choose rail rather than road to visit the National Park, guided walks from several stations and connecting bus services all combined to instantly prove extremely popular, with fully booked trains connecting with buses within the Park and outward into the Lake District. The project was nationally acclaimed, having the unique distinction amongst transport experiments in the National Parks of England and Wales of providing both visitors and the local community with an affordable and integrated transport service.

However, the powerful men at BR headquarters were not convinced, and in 1976 the British Railways Board announced its policy for the years 1976 to 1979 inclusive. On the subject of steam excursions over the main lines, it was announced that no steam would be allowed on the Settle & Carlisle route. This was devastating news, as steam 'specials' during the 1970s had been proving increasingly popular and many saw their continuation as a major factor in the future preservation of the line itself. A predictably hostile response quickly followed, and in 1978 BR changed its mind and agreed to a limited return of steam-hauled excursions over the line. These were an instant success as a result of the tireless efforts of the Steam Locomotive Operators' Association (SLOA), which was formed after the winding up of its predecessor, the Association of Railway Preservation Societies, in 1975. In 1980 BR agreed to the introduction of a train to be called 'The Cumbrian Mountain Express', which would run steam-hauled over the S&C in both directions. Such was the demand for seats on the original programme of six trains (three northbound and three southbound) that the number was doubled to 12.

Flying in the face of this success, 1983 dawned with the jaw-dropping revelation that, in spite of the increasing popularity of the line, BR intended to close the route altogether. The inevitable appearance of official closure proposals in August 1983 provoked a furore of protest from all quarters. Dales Rail users were at the forefront, and more than 20,000 formal objections to closure were received in the designated period, all at a time when the line was busy with additional trains diverted from the West Coast Main Line. Surely the managers could not be so blind to the benefits of this railway? In spite of the dismay, the result was a massive increase in passenger usage of the line. Steam excursions were hugely over-subscribed, and even the normal service trains could not cope, to such an extent that the usual four coaches had to be increased to ten. The world and his wife, it seemed, were clamouring to ride the Long Drag.

For so long BR had deemed the line unprofitable and unpromotable, yet now a remarkable sequence of events was taking place, so much so that two new services were added – a Hull-Carlisle service (at a time when the Leeds-Carlisle trains were regularly full to overflowing with what BR dismissed as 'people taking a last nostalgic trip') and an additional York-Leeds-Carlisle-Leeds-York service, running daily including Sundays. And still the public flocked to travel.

Even the 'die-hards' at BR could no longer ignore the obvious. Not only was the S&C a national treasure in the eyes of the people, it also offered a marketing opportunity that was too attractive to ignore. So in July 1983, just one month before it had intended to publish its intention to seek closure, BR made a major about-turn and issued a promotional leaflet entitled 'Britain's Greatest Historic Scenic Route'.

Still the line's future hung in the balance, as throughout the 1980s the stated policy of BR was to close it. Then came that momentous day, 9 March 1989, when the Minister for Public Transport, Michael Portillo MP, finally stood up in the House of Commons to announce that, because of the weight of new evidence, there would be a 'stay of execution' for the S&C line. An all-party group would be set up to keep the Minister informed of the strength of public opinion and other evidence in support of the line. Immediately, ten further 'Cumbrian Mountain Express' tours were organised by Flying Scotsman Enterprises, all predictably hugely over-subscribed. So it was that Mr Portillo was persuaded: he finally announced that he had refused BR's application to close either the Settle & Carlisle route or the Blackburn to Hellifield line that served it, and further that in future the policy would be that this unique and historic railway would be promoted as a 'BR Leisure Line'.

The future of the line was assured.

Back in 1969, not suspecting such an outcome, I set about photographing this monumental piece of our history. *Riding the Long Drag* is a photographic journey over this magnificent stretch of railway line. Photographs taken from the trains give the passenger's view as the locomotives labour through the often bleak Pennine scenery. Remote signal boxes control our passing, while isolated stations serve scattered communities in lonely dales.

Lineside shots reveal the detail along this unique route and, as the years go by, steam power gradually returns to grace the tracks. The heartbeat of lovingly restored preserved locomotives echoes again across the high moors and life is gradually breathed once more into the unique achievement that is the Settle & Carlisle Railway.

3
Skipton to Settle Junction

For me, travelling as I often did from the industrial heartland of Lancashire, the journey over the S&C began at Skipton station. Here, surrounded by Pennine hills, the first inkling of what lies ahead is revealed. Located at the head of Airedale, in the Craven District of Yorkshire, Skipton itself is sheltered by the heights of Skipton Moor, but the landscape hereabouts has been described as un-English in its bleakness – elemental, the poor, twisted trees, bent by the wind, clinging to jutting crags. There is little cultivation, just moorland, rock outcrops and waterfalls. The weather is rarely welcoming, often dreary in its dampness, and at times downright aggressive.

A brief climb towards Hellifield gives us a taste for what is to come. Before the arrival of the railway in the mid-1840s, Hellifield was just a small hamlet, but with the building of the Settle & Carlisle line in the early 1870s it soon became established as a bustling railway town with a complex of engine sheds and yards. Being at the junction of the Lancashire & Yorkshire and the Midland lines necessitated the housing of a considerable workforce in the immediate area. So the town grew.

Today the station is relatively tranquil, as the busy transfer yards between the 'Lanky' and the Midland have long since gone, and the express passenger trains have been largely replaced by diesel multiple units. The brisk start from Hellifield, with speed

From the train near Skipton in March 1987, the hostile environment of the Yorkshire countryside in winter quickly becomes apparent.

Photographed from the train, waiting in anticipation of departure from Skipton in March 1987.

A look back reminds us of the weather in store in the surrounding hills.

Hellifield station is in an untidy and unkempt condition in 1978, with weeds growing high in the former bay platform. The elaborate maroon and cream ironwork of the canopy, however, reminds us of its glory days with the Midland Railway

The ornate MR ironwork and signal box are clearly visible on 26 July 1978.

Inset: A former Midland Railway water pump gathers rust. Hellifield is sometimes described as a wonderful relic of the Victorian age, referring to the condition of the railway and its run-down buildings. It is in many ways a graveyard of memories.

A DMU for Morecambe comes to a halt at the almost deserted platform at Hellifield on 26 July 1978.

rising rapidly to well over 60mph, is a deceptive opener to a gruelling piece of railway. The gradient then falls away through Long Preston and continues in this easy manner until Settle Junction is approached.

With its smart, typically Midland Railway signal box, with front nameplate, controlling passing traffic for Clapham, Carnforth, Lancaster and Morecambe, as well as for Carlisle, Settle Junction immediately sets the tone for the task ahead, as the challenge of the 1 in 100 climb is

thrown down. This is the 'Long Drag', so named by firemen who sweated up the 25 miles to Ais Gill summit.

The line off to the left here to Clapham is the original route to Carlisle, via Ingleton

Below: Ex-LNER 'K1' No 2005 pilots ex-LMS 'Black 5' No 5407 as they approach Long Preston with the 'Cumbrian Mountain Pullman' in February 1983.

Bottom: In October 1983 No 5407 again approaches Long Preston, this time with the 'Cumbrian Mountain Express'.

More steam at Long Preston: ex-SR 'West Country' Class 'Pacific' No 34092 *City of Wells* storms through the station with the 'Cumbrian Mountain Pullman' in April 1983.

During the same month, on another typically cold and rainy day, ex-LMS No 13809 races through, also with the 'Cumbrian Mountain Pullman'.

over the 'Little North Western'. Opened in 1849, it later joined the Lancaster & Carlisle Railway at Low Gill, south of Tebay, in 1860. This route played a key part in the Midland's decision to lay its own independent rails across the Pennines, for at Ingleton the Midland Railway traffic had to be handed over to the LNWR. The latter's staunch attitude was that companies like the MR should be kept in their place, which it did by making things as awkward as possible for the smaller rival. Accordingly,

Midland traffic often took an incredible time to reach Carlisle via Ingleton. Freight conveyed between Midlands towns and Carlisle regularly took well over a week to arrive, while passengers could find their coaches attached to slow goods trains, or they might be dumped on the bleak platform at Tebay at ghastly hours to await a connection. Long waits and missed connections were commonplace. The situation was clearly intolerable, and so it was that in 1865 the Midland board came to a decision that it must have a line of its own to Carlisle and go all out for a major share of the Anglo-Scottish traffic.

This disturbed the LNWR, which responded by offering attractive incentives to the Midland to abandon its plans; indeed, a Bill of Abandonment was presented to Parliament to that effect, but under pressure from the Lancashire & Yorkshire Railway and the North British Railway, both deeply enthusiastic about

Settle Junction signal box, photographed from the trackside on 17 October 1976.

an independent route to Scotland, the Midland's attempts to extricate itself from its own Act of 1865 were defeated and the project was pushed forward.

The small station just to the south of Settle Junction was probably one of the shortest-lived main-line halts in British railway history. It opened in November 1876 to serve as a traffic exchange point between the new line and the 'Little North Western', and closed exactly one year later in November 1877 after the Midland's Traffic Committee decided that there seemed to be little use for Settle Junction station, as, in their eyes, the 'Little North Western' 'branch' led to nowhere.

Settle Junction signal box, seen from the train as we pass in April 1980.

Ex-LNER 'A4' No 4498 *Sir Nigel Gresley* passes Settle Junction box with the northbound 'Cumbrian Mountain Express' in April 1980.

Ex-LNER 'A3' No 4472 *Flying Scotsman* coasts past the same place with the southbound 'Cumbrian Mountain Express', also in April 1980.

4
Settle to Ribblehead

Settle station is reached soon after the junction. It was lit by gas lamps until 1974, when electricity was finally installed.

The town of Settle is dominated by the towering limestone cliff of Castleberg Crag and is surrounded by moors with spectacular limestone outcrops, caves and waterfalls, making it an excellent base from which to explore this part of the Yorkshire Dales.

Drivers heading over the 'Long Drag' would always hope for a good run through here, and would dread having to attack the gradient from a standing start. The hapless signalman would frequently, though unfairly, be cursed for their ill-fortune. A spirited start from Settle station is required, for the challenge of 1 in 100 is about to be maintained for the next 20 miles, with little respite.

There was a young fireman from the Vale of York who was new to the 'Long Drag'. Confident that he knew his job, he was quite offended when his veteran driver mentioned that the fire might be a little low for the journey ahead. The fireman ignored the comment and turned to admire the Dales scenery. As they passed Craven Quarry near Langcliffe, just north of Settle, the driver quietly pointed out the chimney rising over

Settle station still boasts its maroon name sign in 1979, but for how much longer?

In March 1975 we approach the 'Gothic'-style Settle station. The goods yard and shed have gone, but the water tower remains, now overlooking the car park.

200 feet from the Hoffman Kiln and patiently remarked that 'In next to no time we will be at Ais Gill – the same height as that chimney top.' The fireman looked again – then started shovelling furiously.

All the stations on the Settle & Carlisle except Culgaith were designed by John Holloway Sanders in the style known as 'Derby Gothic'. This was the Midland Railway 'house style' and was used extensively on its network, with grand creations at Derby and, of course, London St Pancras, seen here in February 1978.

In March 1987 we head north through Settle station.

In typically wintry conditions in February 1986 we pass Settle station signal box.

An early evening visit to Settle station on 23 February 1979 is rewarded by the last rays of the sun reflecting off Class 40 No 40013 bringing in a train for Carlisle. After a brief pause, No 40013 gets the signal and heads for the hills.

Passing the church, its cemetery locked in winter's grip, we pick up speed as we head through frozen cuttings north of Settle in March 1987.

Leaving Settle, the railway takes us above the town and out into the unforgiving landscape of the Dales, which in the depths of winter offers a severe test for man and machine.

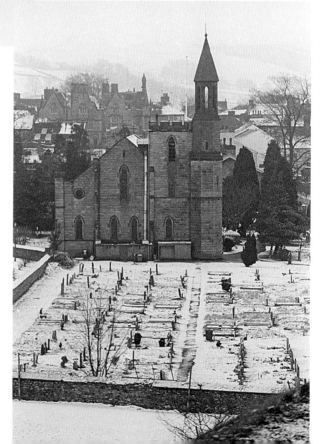

Steadily climbing, we come to Horton-in-Ribblesdale, whose signal box guarded its once decaying station 8 miles from Settle Junction. Horton lies on the Pennine Way and is a favourite starting point for walkers and ramblers for the climb to Pen-y-Ghent. The surrounding area is also well known for its caves and potholes.

Climbing from Settle towards Horton-in-Ribblesdale.

Looking at the state of Horton-in-Ribblesdale station in 1983, it is difficult to believe that in the 1950s and 1960s under Station Master Taylor it won the 'Best Kept Station' award for 17 consecutive years.

In March 1975 our train approaches Horton-in-Ribblesdale station.

Horton signal box is seen on 25 January 1976, the day following O. S. Nock's inspirational talk at Ingleton (see page 12) with, appropriately enough, an engineer's coach parked alongside.

In February 1983 snow falls to welcome the anticipated steam special.

Patience rewarded, through the freezing snow thunders Midland Compound No 1000 piloting ex-LMS 'Jubilee' 4-6-0 No 5690 *Leander*.

Same place, totally different conditions. On a mild afternoon in October 1983, once again we are waiting patiently for a steam special. It is far easier to be patient when the sun is shining, especially when what we are anticipating is a spirited performance from Stanier 'Pacific' No 46229 *Duchess of Hamilton*. We were not disappointed.

Ever onwards and upwards, we climb past the site of Selside signal box, relentlessly tackling the still steep gradient towards Batty Green station and Batty Moss Viaduct – or, as they are more usually known to railway enthusiasts everywhere, Ribblehead station and viaduct. By rail or by road, don't blink or you'll miss the tiny hamlet of Selside, which never did get its promised station. Nearby is the well-known pot-hole, Alum Pot, by the slopes of Simon Fell to the west.

Selside signal box.

A signal box nameplate adorns the village shop.

This is limestone pavement country, much loved by walkers and those interested in the ecology of this unique landscape, typified by the 'clints' (limestone blocks) and 'grykes' (fissures) of Southerscales, near Ribblehead, seen here.

As we climb further into 'Three Peaks' country, Pen-y-Ghent dominates the skyline, with Ingleborough then finally Whernside coming into view to complete the Yorkshire trio.

Unusual among the mountain railways of the world, the Settle & Carlisle is to all intents and purposes straight. What curves do exist are so superbly laid out that in the great days of steam there was not a single speed restriction over the entire length of the route, and Midland expresses could reach speeds of 90mph, matching the average speeds of the LNWR trains over that company's somewhat less gruelling but nevertheless testing route from Lancaster to Carlisle over Shap.

We approach the station at Ribblehead after passing the Salt Lake Cottages, which mark the site of the shanty town of Salt Lake City, with the impressive backdrop of Whernside.

For many years the station master here manned an important weather station,

monitoring the winds that could batter a steam train to a halt between the station and the viaduct. At a height of 1,025 feet above sea level, Ribblehead Viaduct bears the brunt of the fierce winds from the west, which would lift tarpaulins and heave out the contents of wagons, scattering them among the sheep grazing 165 feet below.

Continuing past the Station Inn, appropriately reinforced against the frequent gales, we set forth across the mighty 24-arch viaduct, which was begun in 1870 and took four years to complete.

We are passing what remained of Ribblehead station in March 1975, with Whernside all but hidden in mist and the all too frequent low cloud.

On a brighter day, also in March 1975, we speed past the lonely Station Inn towards the viaduct.

Travelling the line during the early months of the year usually entails braving the elements, which up here means snow. We pass the Station Inn again in February 1986.

Another snowy approach to Ribblehead Viaduct, in March 1987.

5
Ribblehead Viaduct to Dent

As we cross Ribblehead Viaduct we are 13 miles from Settle Junction, and still climbing.

Out here on the moors there were no towns or villages, so the navvies built their own shanty towns during the construction of the line, housing around 2,000 men and their families. The towns were named Sevastopol (in memory of the proud part many navvies had played in the Crimea), Salt Lake City, Jericho and, biggest of all, Batty Green. In St Leonard's churchyard in nearby Chapel-le-Dale, about 2 miles from Ingleton, can be seen a monument to more than 100 unfortunates who died in the construction of the viaduct and nearby Blea Moor Tunnel. The white marble memorial situated on the west wall of the nave reads:

'To the memory of those who through accidents lost their lives in constructing the railway works between Settle and Dent Head. This tablet was erected at the joint expense of their fellow workmen and the Midland Railway Company, 1869-1876.'

The figures speak clearly of the harsh conditions endured by these hardy workmen.

At the well-organised settlement of Batty Green, beside the Ingleton Road, the huts were laid out in regular lines. The location was referred to in early days as 'Batty Wife Hole', some say after the wife of a ne'er-do-well, who sought peace from her suffering by throwing herself into the deep waters of a nearby pothole. The community had its own school and schoolmaster to teach the wild children of wilder parents. It boasted a Mission House with a Missionary, a library, Post Office and a hospital built by the

contractor in 1871, after a smallpox epidemic had claimed 80 lives.

Between 1869 and 1877, together with the viaducts at Arten Gill, Dent Head and Smardale, and Dent station itself, Ribblehead Viaduct was built under the watchful eye of Engineer-in-Charge John Sydney Crossley. A Leicestershire man, he brought his knowledge and experience as a veteran of other Midland schemes to overcome the challenges of this unique route, supervising the construction of these sturdy structures built to stand the test of time.

One yarn tells of a navvy who was blown off the top, through an arch and back onto the viaduct again. Records do confirm that, such was the strength of the wind, one goods train of 40 wagons lost the loads of all but five of them as it crossed the viaduct in a gale, and more recently freight lost over the side has included several cars.

However, 100 years of exposure to gales of up to 120mph accompanied by horizontal rain were causing the mighty limestone piers to crumble at an alarming rate. The *Yorkshire Post* of 19 May 1981, under the headline 'Bridge future on the line', described the thoughts of BR's then Divisional Civil Engineer, Alan King, who listed the mounting problems associated with maintaining the viaduct. He concluded that 'It would cost as much to permanently repair as it would to replace'. However, a new bridge would present more than engineering problems. Quite apart from having to close the line for an estimated three years (at a time when it carried up to 40 trains a day and served as an important diversion when the regular weekend engineering work rendered the West Coast Main Line

These two view were taken from trains approaching the viaduct in February 1986 and March 1987. Since 1984 the line has reduced to a single track in an attempt to limit further damage to the stonework.

From below the towering arches on Batty Moss, the full impressive structure can be appreciated. In May 1989 Ribblehead Viaduct still stands impressively, 115 years after completion.

Far above the heads of the grazing sheep, the track is held firm.

An LMS rail chair dated '4 29', photographed in March 1975, bears witness to the line's long and distinguished history.

An unidentified 'Peak' approaches the viaduct from the north on the same day.

unavailable), Parliamentary approval would be needed and permission to demolish the existing viaduct, listed as an historic monument, could prove complex. Rumour had it that BR, faced with the massive cost of maintaining the viaduct, planned to fill in the arches and replace the centre span with a pre-cast concrete structure. It is not difficult to imagine what Mr Crossley would have thought of this violation.

Leaving Ribblehead Viaduct in March 1975 on board the train for Carlisle.

Now we have left the towering structure of Ribblehead Viaduct behind us, arching as it does across the wild high moors, the train crew could anticipate some respite from the gruelling climb as Blea Moor is approached and, beyond it, more favourable gradients, for a while…

The isolated signal box at Blea Moor controls the entrance to the lengthy Blea Moor Tunnel, which runs for 2,629 dark yards some 500 feet beneath the fells. So remote is the box that water supplies have to be delivered every day by train!

The top of Blea Moor stands at an altitude of 1,753 feet, and at this height in the Pennines in winter conditions for man

Looking towards Blea Moor from the trackside.

The isolated signal box at Blea Moor, seen in March 1975.

and machine are at their most challenging. In steam days the exhaust beats of labouring locomotives could be heard long before they appeared on the curve approaching the viaduct, while across the open moor the sound of the wind and the haunting, warbling call of the curlew would soon be overwhelmed in a mass of steam, smoke and thunder.

For the signalman at remote Blea Moor, the nearest car parking is under the viaduct at Ribblehead, about a mile away. A pleasant enough walk in summer, but not so appealing in winter!

When snow comes to these parts, as it often does, the harsh landscape can become decidedly inhospitable. It's February 1986 and the remoteness and sense of isolation is felt even from the comfort of the train. As we travel through the white landscape surrounding Blea Moor signal box, now having lost its water tower and some outbuildings, the signalman watches our train pass on its way to Carlisle, as generations before him have done for more than 100 years. On the train, few enthusiasts brave the freezing conditions to record the passing scene, as the power of the Class 45 diesel is tested further. The engine's throbbing tone deepens as we pass the signal box and head onwards, still at 1 in 100, towards the summit of this section, inside the tunnel itself.

Approaching Blea Moor signal box in March 1987, passing the up goods line signal, the speed restriction sign for the viaduct, then the famous box itself.

In more clement conditions, this is the view from the footpath up to the box from the viaduct, in March 1975.

The isolation of Blea Moor signal box can be appreciated more fully when looking back from the bridge carrying the path over the fells. The flat top of Ingleborough looms in the distance.

Abandoning the train for a few moments and following the footpath from Ribblehead Viaduct, past Blea Moor signal box and up onto the open moor, we reach the gaping mouth of Blea Moor Tunnel, an enormously expensive undertaking. Digging the tunnel cost £45 a yard, and there were 2,629 of them! This and other spiralling costs meant that the entire railway project took more than half as much again to complete as the original £2.2 million budget.

To feed the workforce in these wild places, beef, the preferred meat, arrived 'on the hoof'. The more easily available mutton was despised, and bacon was eaten only to 'fill in the cracks'. Other supplies arrived on carts that had to run on barrels rather than ordinary wheels, which would sink hopelessly up to their axles. These 'bog-carts' would need three horses to haul them, and even then the horses would often need to be heaved bodily out of the thick gluey mire.

The high rate of pay, 10 shillings per day, was barely sufficient enticement for many navvies to stay long in these treacherous working conditions. Even though at any one time the workforce might number 2,000 men, overall more than 33,000 came, stayed a while, then 'jacked'.

The navvies, working by candlelight, hacked out this amazing feat of engineering with picks, shovels, gunpowder and sweat. Working in appalling conditions of severe hardship for more than 12 hours a day, six days a week, took its toll, and in winter many never saw daylight for almost a week at a time.

In the shanty towns the navvies ate, drank and fought. Heavy drinking on Saturday nights heralded a 'Day of Rest' on Sundays, as the 'Lord's Day' was observed. For many, though, Sunday was also 'Fight Day', when contenders battled it out bare-knuckled for the title 'Cock of the Camp'. The champion might then be matched against a professional fighter brought in for the occasion. Thus the camps became notorious.

The walk onto the fell runs parallel with the railway until the cart-track bridge over the line, where Blea Moor's Distant signal stands at the southern end of the tunnel. Beyond the tunnel, the footpath continues to the summit of Whernside. Above the tunnel mouth you can still make out the spoil heaps where the excavation material from the tunnel was tipped.

In early 1975 the old Blea Moor Tunnel sign was replaced. The old one can be seen as our train plunges into the tunnel in March of that year, while the inset shows the old sign lying discarded below the new a few weeks later.

Blea Moor Tunnel is an assault on the senses. Light is extinguished quickly and totally, while sound is magnified and the cold dank smell fills the nostrils.

Looking back out of the tunnel, and it's snowing again…

Emerging into Dentdale at the north end of Blea Moor Tunnel.

At last the challenging gradient eases and we leave the depths of Blea Moor Tunnel and roll down into beautiful Dentdale – what a contrast!

Dentdale is one of the most secluded of the Yorkshire Dales, stretching 14 miles from Whernside to Sedbergh. Dent is known locally as Dent Town, and is the only village in the Dale. A lovely collection of cottages and delightful cobbled streets, it has existed since Norman times, though there is some evidence that the Romans once occupied the Dale.

The limestone of the area is responsible for another of the Dale's attractions, caving. The complex system of caverns and underground passages attracts cavers from far afield, and the geological phenomena associated with the 'Dent Fault' were instrumental in focusing Adam Sedgewick's early studies in the new science of geology.

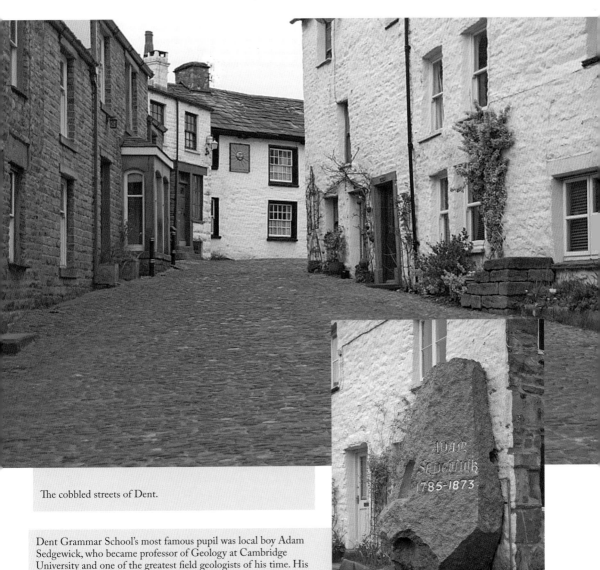

The cobbled streets of Dent.

Dent Grammar School's most famous pupil was local boy Adam Sedgewick, who became professor of Geology at Cambridge University and one of the greatest field geologists of his time. His pink granite memorial encloses a water fountain, the village supply in the days before piped water was available.

Dent station was reopened to passengers in 1986 and, at 1,150 feet above sea level, is the highest main-line station in England. It is more than 4 miles from the village in the valley below that bears its name, a distance that led to the now famous wisecrack:

Visitor: 'Why did they build Dent station so far from the village?'
Local: ''Appen they wanted it near t' railway lines.'

The nearby Arten Gill Viaduct is constructed from massive blocks of stone known as 'Dent Marble', hewn from now disused quarries in the Dale. It is a black limestone rich in the fossilised remains of crinoids, sea creatures related to the starfish and sea urchins. From the late 18th century polished Dent Marble was used to make beautiful fireplaces that adorned fashionable Victorian homes, thanks to the services of the new railway; several examples still remain in the old houses in the Dale.

Dent Station signal box. Before worries about 'carbon footprints' and global warming, the box boasts a sizeable pile of coal on 28 March 1975.

Looking south from the station past the box, Dent
Head Viaduct can be seen in the distance.

It's Sunday and the box is closed, but a view through the window reveals the levers set for the signals and points at 'all clear'.

Dent Station signal box is seen from a train to Carlisle in March 1975, with the station master's house in the background. The highest such house in England, it was protected against the severe weather by having slates fastened over three of its outside walls and, uniquely for the time, double-glazed windows.

The station is seen looking south in 1973 from the bridge carrying the old 'Coal Road', used to access the small open-cast coal mines that were once worked in the area. It climbs over the fells to Garsdale, and is itself an interesting journey, treacherous in bad weather, with gradients of 1 in 5. It carries its own warning, somewhat understated, advising that this unclassified road, at an altitude of 1,759 feet, 'can be dangerous'!

Being a Sunday, the box is closed and the signals have been left 'off', to allow the sparse traffic to pass through the section unhindered. Above the platform can be seen the remains of the double line of snow fences, erected from old railway sleepers to protect the station from the worst of the winter snow.

Another view looking south from the station, in July 1977.

From the station, the fine vista of beautiful Dentdale can be readily appreciated, even when the all too frequent low cloud limits visibility and the village of Dent is lost in the misty distance.

On 22 October 1978 preserved 'A4' 'Pacific' No 4498 *Sir Nigel Gresley*, chime whistle sounding, races through Dent with 'The Moorlander' special from Carlisle.

6
Garsdale to Ais Gill

Compared to the testing gradients behind us, the 10 miles or so to Ais Gill are something of a stroll. The line is now at an altitude of more than 1,000 feet and the landscape of the high fells brings plenty of interest. The climb, however, is not over yet.

After passing under the Coal Road at Dent and travelling through a short cutting we plunge into the darkness of Rise Hill Tunnel.

The southern portal of the remote Rise Hill Tunnel in March 1975. This was one of the last and most difficult to build of the line's structures. Sadly, 100 years after completion the process of replacing the old signs, with their cast-iron letters screwed onto a wooden board, slowly dismantles another piece of railway history.

From Rise Hill Tunnel we emerge into the long straight valley of Garsdale, with the railway running on a ledge high above the valley floor.

This stretch of line once boasted the highest water troughs in the world. A quarter of a mile long and fed by a massive 43,000-gallon water tank that collected water off the fells, the troughs were once steam-heated to protect against winter frosts. To this day, watering facilities are provided to quench the thirst of the labouring steam locomotives employed on the ever-popular 'specials'.

Garsdale station was once the junction for the 6-mile branch to Hawes, famed as the home of Wensleydale cheese. Then known as Hawes Junction, the station was equipped with a unique stockaded turntable, shielding locomotives from the fierce winds that might otherwise have spun the helpless engine and her crew.

It was from Hawes Junction on Christmas Eve 1910 that Signalman Alfred Sutton dispatched a pair of light engines onto the main line, and unwittingly caused the deaths of 12 people in the ensuing crash and blaze. The Midland had gained a reputation for being one of the most highly organised railways in Britain, yet its 'small engine' policy meant that the majority of trains needed pilot engine assistance up both sides of the 'big hump'. Thus it was on that wild and pitch-black night near the summit of the 'Long Drag' that no fewer than five light engines were being held prior to turning and running back to Carlisle or Leeds, and through traffic was also busy, though this was not unusual.

Signalman Sutton allowed two light engines coupled together to come off the turntable road and onto the main line, there to be held at the signal. They waited for more than 10 minutes as the weather did its worst, and the signalman forgot about them. Eventually Sutton was offered and accepted the midnight 'sleeper' from St Pancras to Glasgow, which, though running late, was valiantly striving to make up time. The signals were pulled off for the express, and the light engine crews assumed this was for them and set off towards Carlisle.

Only after emerging from Moorcock Tunnel, a short distance down the line, did the fireman of the rear loco realise what was happening, but too late, as the heavier train appeared right behind and smashed into them at speed. The wooden carriages splintered upon impact and the gas lighting set off an inferno as the train left the tracks.

Signalman Sutton, looking north from his box, realised the sickening reality of what he had done as he saw the glare of light turning the sky crimson over Ais Gill. He could do nothing but humbly ask his relief signalman, who had just arrived, to tell the station master, 'I am afraid I have wrecked the Scotch Express.'

In this remote country, pubs are few and far between, so the isolated Moorcock Inn provides welcome respite for those hardy folk who travel in these parts and who may well have the place virtually to themselves. At the junction of the A684 Hawes-Sedburgh road and the B6259 to Kirkby Stephen, the Moorcock dates back to the 1840s. It stands alone, the only hostelry for 15 long and lonely miles.

It was in the pub's cellar that the bodies of the 12 victims of the Hawes Junction tragedy were stored, prior to their burial in the small churchyard at Hawes, and here that the preliminary inquiry into the accident was convened. In this October 1985 picture, sunlight streams into the bar.

The tragedy, caused as it was by a combination of human error and failure to follow railway rules relating to trains standing at signals, triggered an inquiry that stressed the need to install electric lighting in coaching stock, highlighted the value of the use of signal lever collars to remind signalmen which lines were occupied, and was instrumental in the eventual introduction of the newly invented system of track-circuiting.

On a sunny summer day in June 1975 our train comes to a halt at the charming station of Garsdale.

A glimpse through the window of Garsdale signal box in July 1977 reveals the world of the signalman containing a few basic comforts. Dandry Mire Viaduct can be seen in the distance.

Garsdale station has been the preferred watering stop in the high fells, and thus provides opportunities to get close to the locomotives hauling the special trains, though at times the weather tries its best to thwart the photographer's best-laid plans. Preserved SR 'Merchant Navy' 'Pacific' No 35028 *Clan Line* takes water in the thick fog at Garsdale station on 23 September 1978.

Below and right: A 'Duchess' at Garsdale: ex-LMS Stanier 'Pacific' No 46229 *Duchess of Hamilton* waits at Garsdale, then makes a spirited departure in October 1985.

Another view of
Garsdale signal box, in
July 1977.

As we leave Garsdale in
February 1984, only the pit
of the turntable remains.

The final assault on the summit begins shortly after leaving Garsdale station, with a stiff climb through the short Moorcock Tunnel, over Lund's Viaduct, then on through Shotlock Hill Tunnel towards Ais Gill itself.

Photographed from the train in March 1975, we enter Shotlock Hill Tunnel, and the old sign is still in place.

A very short time later that same month the sign lies on the trackside, having been unceremoniously replaced.

Shotlock Hill Tunnel, like the other feats of engineering along this most arduous of routes, was constructed to withstand the worst that the weather could inflict upon it, and has survived all these years, as evidenced by the date, 1875, on the southern portal.

Once through Shotlock Hill Tunnel, the summit of the line is soon reached. Ais Gill, at a height of 1,169 feet above sea level, is a uniquely remote spot for a signal box, with the mighty bulk of Wild Boar Fell overshadowing the line, but it did perform the vital function of guarding the refuge sidings here in the days when pilot engines were detached at the summit before being sent to Garsdale for turning.

Approaching Ais Gill in March 1975, a Class 40 passes southbound at speed.

Seen from the same train, we pass Ais Gill signal box with a rather ominous-looking wagon parked outside. Was this merely delivering the coal, or was it left, like a skip, to collect the remains of the famous box as it was demolished?

Photographed from the same train again, we pass Ais Gill's Up Distant signal.

Ais Gill signal box in June 1975.

The summit signs in June 1975 and October 1985. Signs such as this were essential in the days of double-headed trains; to allow the pilot engine to be uncoupled, drivers had to be sure that they had taken their train beyond the top, and not left it 'hanging over the edge', where its weight could easily drag the locomotive backwards down the hill again.

The back of the signal box in 1969, the door open to let in the warm summer air.

Through the window in 1972.

Reaching the top with steam: on 22 October 1978 'A4' 'Pacific' No 4498 *Sir Nigel Gresley* passes Ais Gill box with 'The Moorlander', heading south.

In October 1983, the vast scale of the Pennine landscape becomes apparent as 'Duchess' 'Pacific' No 46229 *Duchess of Hamilton* storms through the Mallerstang Valley towards the summit from Carlisle and (*inset opposite*) reaches her goal as she thunders through Ais Gill.

The 'Cumbrian Mountain Pullman' reaches Ais Gill summit in November 1983, with *Duchess of Hamilton* again in charge. In October 1985 the 'Duchess' eases 'The Caledonian' over the top.

The end of an era at Ais Gill: on 22 October 1978 the nameboard is missing; passing in November 1981 the box is partly demolished; and by the freezing February of 1984 it has gone.

7
On to Appleby

Steam engines seemed to breathe a sigh of relief as they crested the summit. The battle against the gradient has lasted for more than 25 miles, but once Ais Gill is behind us it is downhill virtually all the way to Carlisle. Our way lies through the beautiful Eden Valley, in the lee of Wild Boar Fell, so named because it is reputedly the place where the last wild boar in England was killed.

The famous 'helm' wind of winter races up and down Eden Dale in fierce flurries, often remarkably local in their effects, once tearing an anemometer clean away from its moorings. When the signs appeared in the form of a 'helmet' of cloud like a black bar running the length of the valley above the escarpment, the message to railwaymen was usually limited to two brief words: 'Secure sheets!' The 'gale-men', constantly on call, would respond accordingly by checking and retightening the tarpaulins that covered and protected the wagons' cargo.

Gradually we descend into the Mallerstang Valley, where the lonely signal box was closed as early as 1969 and subsequently destroyed by fire. In the opposite direction this too is a steep and unrelenting climb, but heading north we can relax and enjoy the impressive Pennine scenery as we roll down towards Appleby.

Nearby is the village of Outhgill where, in the early 18th century, blacksmith James Faraday became father to a son, Michael, destined to become a world-renowned physicist and now immortalised in the unit of electrical capacitance, the Farad.

Also nearby are the remains of the 12th-century Pendragon Castle, reputed to be the home of Uther Pendragon, father of the legendary King Arthur.

Near Crosby Garratt is a favoured lineside spot from which to capture dramatic shots of southbound trains attacking the 1 in 100 gradient. The railway passes the village by means of Smardale Viaduct, whose six arches overshadow the small cluster of homes and farms grouped around a beck, nestling amongst the Howgills and the northern Pennines, 3 miles west of Kirkby Stephen.

Coasting downhill, we pass the site of Griseburn Ballast Sidings signal box near Crosby Garratt, the halfway point on the Settle & Carlisle line, and a fine setting to appreciate the full sweep of the lovely Eden Valley. The Midland Railway's sidings, built to serve the nearby quarries, were closed in 1970.

Next we plunge into Helm Tunnel near the village of Helm, from where the wild wind gets its name.

We now arrive at Appleby, the former county town of Westmorland, a position it

'A4' 'Pacific' No 4498 *Sir Nigel Gresley* pounds up the gradient near Crosby Garratt with the southbound 'Cumbrian Mountain Express' in January 1980.

Griseburn Ballast Sidings signal box, near Crosby Garratt.

An 1899 Midland Railway trespass notice photographed at Appleby Station in 1974.

held until Westmorland disappeared into Cumbria in 1974, by which time Kendal had become a greater centre of activity.

Appleby-in-Westmorland is the only large town on the entire route from Settle to Carlisle, and boasts a fine station and signal box. It is interesting to note, then, that more navvies camped and laboured to build Ribblehead Viaduct and Blea Moor Tunnel than the current population of Appleby.

Appleby enjoys a milder and drier climate than neighbouring areas due to its sheltered position between the high Pennines to the east and the Lakeland fells to the west. Given its strategic position in the Eden Valley, it became the key market town of Westmorland after the Norman Conquest. Since then it has developed into an attractive and picturesque community, with its unusually wide main street, Boroughgate, having

Appleby station, its name set in stones in March 1975.

Still sporting an LMS bridge plate, March 1975.

been described as one of the finest in England. At its high end is Appleby Castle, formerly owned by the Kings of England as well as being seized by the King of Scotland. It was once the home of that great lady of Westmorland and devout Christian, Lady Anne Clifford, who famously restored churches, almshouses and castles to their former glory; these included the castles at Skipton and Pendragon, as well as Appleby Castle itself.

Appleby's other claim to fame is the Horse Fair. This was set up by a Charter granted by James II in 1685 as a fair for horse-trading that runs for a week ending on the second Wednesday in June. Today it is famous as the largest of its kind in the world and attracts a huge gathering, prompting the closure of the road from Appleby to Brampton for the duration. This allows sellers to show off their horses to potential buyers by trotting them up and down the roadway. Each day, prior to this, the horses are led down to the River Eden in the town centre to be washed and groomed ready for the day's trading.

The station footbridge also carried its own LMS bridge plate, number 236A, as seen on 21 April 1976.

Although the town centre boasts many fine pubs, the Midland Hotel, by the station, is a great place for a drink and a sandwich while waiting for your train.

In memory of Bishop Eric Treacy, the 'Railway Bishop'

On 13 May 1978 Eric Treacy left his home, The Ghyll, in the village of Applethwaite, just outside Keswick, to travel to Appleby in order to photograph one of his favourite locomotives, 9F No 92220 *Evening Star*.

After slipping and falling on the wet footbridge steps on the station, he quickly picked himself up and carried on, but a short time later he collapsed and died, having suffered a major coronary attack.

In a rare tribute, Class 86/2 electric locomotive No 86240, which had worked 'The Lord Bishop' memorial train from Euston to Preston, was later named *Bishop Eric Treacy*.

He is buried at St Kentigern's church, Crusthwaite, Keswick.

Eric Treacy where he loved to be, amongst railway folk, as seen here at Haworth station on the Keighley & Worth Valley Railway in 1972. He is quoted as being of the opinion that the three major man-made wonders of the world are York Minster, Hadrian's Wall and the Settle & Carlisle Railway.

A memorial service for the 'Railway Bishop' was fixed for 30 September and three of his favourite locomotives were involved, LNER 'A3' No 4472 *Flying Scotsman*, SR 'Merchant Navy' No 35028 *Clan Line* and, most appropriately, BR Class 9F No 92220 *Evening Star*. Thereby more than 1,000 people were taken to Appleby, and by the time the memorial service started well over 4,000 were in the congregation on the platforms, where a 1-minute silence was started and ended by the whistle of *Evening Star*.

On 30 September 1978 special commemorative trains hauled by Nos 4472 *Flying Scotsman*, 35028 *Clan Line* and 92220 *Evening Star* brought a congregation to Appleby where, after the memorial service, a memorial plaque was unveiled in loving memory of the 'Railway Bishop'.

Eric Treacy was famous not only for his love of railways, but also for his many evocative photographs of steam locomotives throughout Britain. In his memory, special trains ran over his beloved Settle & Carlisle line on 30 September 1978. Seen here are preserved 'A3' 'Pacific' No 4472 *Flying Scotsman*, climbing past Crosby Garratt with the southbound 'The Bishop Treacy', and preserved 'Merchant Navy' 'Pacific' No 35028 *Clan Line* passing the same spot with 'The Lord Bishop', both heading for Appleby.

Evening Star's footplate crew talk with members of the congregation at Appleby station following the service in memory of Bishop Treacy. The inset shows the 9F preparing to leave.

Other steam at Appleby: No 4498 *Sir Nigel Gresley* pauses for water with the 'Cumbrian Mountain Express' in January 1980.

Sir Nigel Gresley departs from Appleby having been watered in the siding near the signal box.

8
Appleby to Carlisle

As we head out from the station we pass Appleby North Junction signal box. Penrith and Kirkby Stephen were once connected to the Durham coalfield via the former North Eastern Railway line, but now the only reminder of Penrith Junction is the empty sidings.

Appleby North Junction signal box in November 1981.

Another view of the junction, with the line to the former
NER Kirkby Stephen-Penrith route on the right.

In contrast to the dramatic scenery of the
past 45 miles, we now encounter a gentler
landscape of farmland interspersed with
forest and permeated by rivers. As we speed
onwards towards Culgaith we experience
a section of level running, in fact the
longest such track on the line. Culgaith is a
straggling village in the Eden Valley, with
the popular walking area of Cross Fell to the
east. It dates back to Medieval times, but
undoubtedly owes its survival to the railway.

It is also the location of a rare level
crossing on this tortuous route across the

Speeding through the gentler landscape near Culgaith.

Culgaith Crossing box, seen in March 1975.

backbone of England. Culgaith Crossing box controls the first of only two road crossings on the entire line, the second being Low House Crossing on the approach to Carlisle. The architecturally unique station at Culgaith had platforms made of wood, a resource plentiful in this locality.

Passing through Culgaith Tunnel and the shorter Waste Bank Tunnel, we encounter the graceful River Eden close to the line on the left.

The gentle Eden Valley spreads before us, welcoming us back to the lowlands and beckoning us onwards to Carlisle.

Approaching Carlisle, Petterill Bridge Junction sees the end of the Midland's route to the North. The final short section to Citadel station is over former NER metals from Newcastle, which join the LNWR main line before we ease under the canopy of Carlisle Citadel station itself.

The border city of Carlisle, situated just 9 miles from Scotland, is located at the western end of the eponymous wall erected by Emperor Hadrian between AD 122

Petterill Bridge Junction seen from behind No 45118 as it heads our train, the 09.07 from Leeds, in February 1984.

and 128 as the limit of the Roman Empire. Becoming an English city in 1092 after a period in Scottish hands, Carlisle has had a history of capture and recapture, the last incursion having been that of Bonnie Prince Charlie in 1745.

Carlisle Citadel station was the meeting point of lines operated by no fewer than seven railway companies (eight, if the Furness is included): the Newcastle & Carlisle, from 1836; the Maryport & Carlisle; the Lancaster & Carlisle; the Caledonian; the Glasgow & South Western; the North British; and finally, in 1876, the Midland. Only London had more railway companies entering its city. To add to the complexity and confusion, each used its own locos and goods facilities.

The station itself was owned and operated by the Lancaster & Carlisle Railway (later becoming part of the London & North Western Railway) and the Caledonian Railway, which set up the Carlisle Citadel Station Committee (CCSC) to manage the running of traffic and trains in the station

area. The other five railway companies were tenants in the station.

On joining this 'club', the Midland found that it had more major obstacles to overcome. The station was in the hands of rival companies, and accusations flew that those two major players had rigged station running arrangements and signalling in their favour and at the expense of the Midland and her allies, the Glasgow & South Western and the North British. Lengthy negotiations resulted in the Midland camp being granted basic rights at Carlisle, and the CCSC was duly enlarged to accommodate the newcomer.

In order to allow this potential bottleneck to be negotiated as efficiently as possible, and so that no goods traffic passed through the station, an elaborate system of avoiding lines was built to the west in 1877 to bypass Citadel. No fewer than four engine sheds catered for the mass of locomotives

No 45118 rests at Carlisle, having successfully brought our train over the 'Long Drag'.

that served the lines radiating from this hub. Kingmoor was originally built by the Caledonian and supplied the route to Glasgow and the North; Upperby was responsible for the prestigious southbound trains to London, as well as those for Penrith and Keswick and to West Cumberland; the old Midland shed at Durranhill looked after locos for the Settle & Carlisle line and the nearby mines and quarries; and Canal shed of the North British serviced the 'Waverley Route' traffic to Edinburgh, as well as trains for Newcastle and the Silloth branch. The situation was eased by restructuring the lines, and a rebuilt Citadel station came into use on 4 July 1880.

However, the increasingly chaotic situation in the goods yards eventually necessitated the building of vast new marshalling yards at Kingmoor. Opened in 1963, these greatly eased the congestion, allowing much rationalisation of goods handling. The end of steam in 1968 and the closure of the 'Waverley Route' in 1969 led to further reductions in traffic, including the closure of the original goods line – the Canal Branch – after more than 130 years.

So we reach the end of the line, after a journey through railway history, one that surely must be preserved as a national treasure. This is no branch line. It was engineered for high-speed running throughout. It followed the natural pathways through the hills of the Pennines to compete for Anglo-Scottish traffic. As a result, the local population was never well served.

It was the last main-line railway in England to be constructed almost entirely by hand. Hundreds of navvies lost their lives building it due to accidents, fights or disease; on completion it was advertised as 'the most picturesque route to Scotland', and the Victorian and Edwardian travelling public took it to their hearts. Thus it played an important role in the developing fortunes of the Midland Railway Company.

Preserved EE Type 4 No D200 stands outside Carlisle station in February 1986.

In February 1984 electric loco No 86209 *City of Coventry* – in the minds of steam enthusiasts a name for ever associated with 'Duchess' No 46240 – waits to take her train south on the West Coast Main Line, the route of the 'Duchesses'.

Back in June 1975 Nos 86010 and 86101 wait on the centre roads at Carlisle for their next duty.

A carriage window notice proudly proclaims that 'named trains' still grace the West Coast Main Line in April 1976 – the S&C had lost its 'Thames-Clyde Express' the previous year.

The old station control room at Citadel with its viewing platform, seen in April 1976.

Carlisle

Photographed in the gloom of the station on 26 May 1975, and carrying the accumulated soot and grime of well over 100 years of passing trains, this Carlisle Citadel Station Committee bridge plate No 4 is one of the very few ever made.

The remains of Carlisle Upperby shed's roundhouse, to the south of the station, photographed on 28 May 1975.

Another closure associated with the area, that of the Haltwhistle to Alston branch of the Tyne Valley line between Carlisle and Newcastle, was notified to the travelling public by means of this poster on Carlisle station platform, photographed on 21 April 1976.

BRITISH RAIL
PUBLIC NOTICE : TRANSPORT ACT 1962

Passenger Services

HALTWHISTLE TO ALSTON

On and from Monday 3 May 1976 the passenger services between Haltwhistle and Alston will be withdrawn and the following passenger stations closed:

Featherstone Park	Slaggyford
Coanwood	Alston
Lambley	

An additional alternative bus service will be provided by Ribble Motor Services on behalf of Northumberland County Council and they will issue timetable details at a later date.

British Rail Eastern

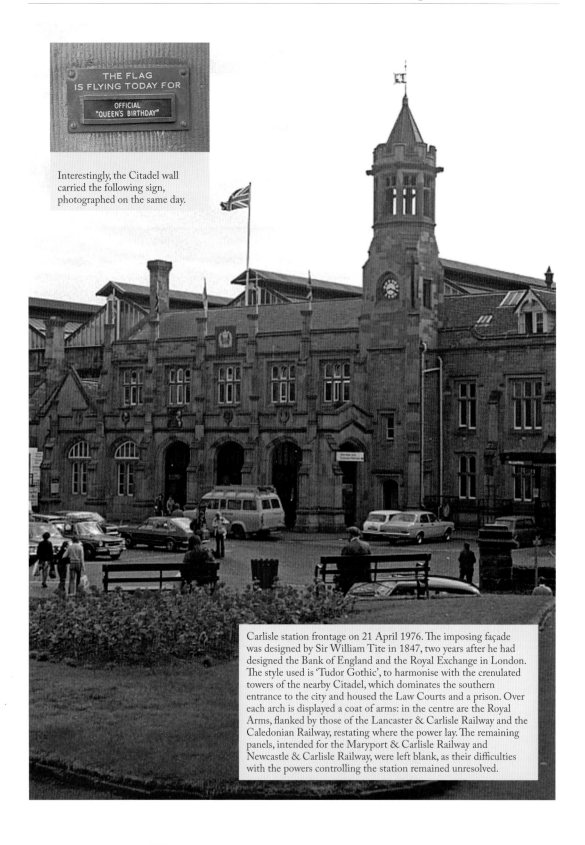

THE FLAG
IS FLYING TODAY FOR

OFFICIAL
"QUEEN'S BIRTHDAY"

Interestingly, the Citadel wall
carried the following sign,
photographed on the same day.

Carlisle station frontage on 21 April 1976. The imposing façade
was designed by Sir William Tite in 1847, two years after he had
designed the Bank of England and the Royal Exchange in London.
The style used is 'Tudor Gothic', to harmonise with the crenulated
towers of the nearby Citadel, which dominates the southern
entrance to the city and housed the Law Courts and a prison. Over
each arch is displayed a coat of arms: in the centre are the Royal
Arms, flanked by those of the Lancaster & Carlisle Railway and the
Caledonian Railway, restating where the power lay. The remaining
panels, intended for the Maryport & Carlisle Railway and
Newcastle & Carlisle Railway, were left blank, as their difficulties
with the powers controlling the station remained unresolved.

Appendix 1
'Inspired leadership and dogged determination'

Typical of the flair and vision that pervaded the Midland Railway's management style was its decision to abolish 2nd Class travel – a stroke of genius.

In 1874 the company's board took the 'revolutionary' decision, which would radically change the face of railway travel from that time on and, though fiercely opposed by its rivals, would prove a major attraction to the travelling public. It was announced that from 1 January 1875 'all the benefits hitherto exclusively enjoyed by the First Class passenger would be bestowed henceforth also upon the Second Class'. The decision was made even more popular by declaring that all were to be carried at 2nd Class fare prices. This, together with substantial improvements made in 3rd Class carriages – cushioned seats, separate compartments, greater space and foot-warmers for winter, elevated rail travel to new heights of comfort. The overall effect was that the railway system had never been so popular. Millions of Midland Railway passengers now travelled in greater comfort than ever before, while paying far lower fares. This momentous decision was born out of the rapidly increasing productiveness of the 3rd Class traffic, while fewer and fewer passengers opted for 2nd Class.

The figures for 1873 on the Midland system tell the story: 1st Class passengers accounted for 5% of those carried and generated 16% of the income, but there was increasing evidence that the well-to-do were shunning 1st Class in favour of travelling at the much cheaper 3rd Class rates. The figures for 2nd Class were 11% of passengers, yet only 15% of income, while 3rd Class had leapt to 84% of passengers carried, generating 69% of the total fares paid.

The case for change was clear. Most passengers preferred 3rd Class, while 2nd Class carriages remained empty and thus formed an increasingly large proportion of 'dead weight' on the trains. The loss of some revenue at the more expensive end would, the board calculated, be more than compensated for by the increased attractiveness of rail travel for the wider public. This, together with the prospect of more economical shorter trains, convinced the Directors of the wisdom of this revolutionary action.

How right they were. The Midland Railway prospered as never before.

Appendix 2
Historical note

Of the signal boxes featured in the text, Settle Junction, Blea Moor, Garsdale, Appleby North and Culgaith Crossing are still open.

Those closed are Settle Station, in May 1984 (moved from its original position and restored to display condition by the Friends of the Settle & Carlisle Railway); Horton-in-Ribblesdale, also in May 1984 (burned down shortly afterwards 'in mysterious circumstances'); Selside, in November 1975 (which during the Second World War was the only main-line box in Britain manned by women, and has now been re-erected and preserved at Steamtown Railway Centre, Carnforth); Dent Station, in January 1981; and Ais Gill, in February 1981 (which was never completely demolished after closure, and was removed and transported to the Midland Railway Centre at Butterley, Derbyshire, for renovation).

Selside signal box is preserved at Steamtown Railway Centre, Carnforth; preserved 'Black 5' No 45407 passes in April 1977.

Of the stations featured in the text, Settle has been refurbished to include a shop operated by the Friends of the Settle & Carlisle Railway; Horton-in-Ribblesdale station was refurbished during 1999 and is now almost back to its former glory; Ribblehead station was refurbished and reopened with a visitor centre in 2000; Dent station was reopened to passenger traffic in 1986 and has since been refurbished; Garsdale station has been refurbished and still boasts a fully operational signal box; the turntable at Garsdale was recovered in 1989 and restored by volunteers to work again on the Keighley & Worth Valley Railway; and Appleby station has been refurbished and boasts the longest platforms on the line, at 200 yards, built originally to accommodate the Anglo-Scottish expresses.

Life is being breathed back into the 'Long Drag' after all…

Bibliography

Baughan, Peter E. *The Midland Railway North of Leeds* (1987; Guild Publishing)

Coleman, T. *The Railway Navvies* (1965; Book Club Associates)

Dorman, G. G. *Carlisle [Citadel] Railway Scene* (1972; George Allen & Unwin)

Ellis, C. Hamilton *The Midland Railway* (1966; Ian Allan)

Flinders, T. G. *On the Settle & Carlisle Route* (1981; Ian Allan)
     The Settle & Carlisle Route Revisited (1985; Ian Allan)

Houghton, Frederick W. and Foster, W. Hubert *The Story of the Settle-Carlisle Line* (1965; The Advertiser Press)

Joy, David and Mitchell, W. R. *Settle-Carlisle Centenary* (1975; Dalesman)

Mitchell, W. R. and Joy, David *Settle to Carlisle: A Railway over the Pennines* (1982; Dalesman)
     Settle-Carlisle Railway (1973; Dalesman)

Nock, O. S. and Cross, Derek *Main Lines Across the Border* (1982; Ian Allan)

Nock, O. S. *From the Footplate* (1984; Guild Publishing)
     Historic Railway Disasters (1970; Arrow Books)

Peart-Binns, John S. *Eric Treacy* (1980; Ian Allan)

Robinson, Peter W. *Railways of Cumbria* (1980; Dalesman)

Rolt, L. T. C. *Red for Danger* (1966; Pan Books)

Siviter, R. *The Settle to Carlisle: A Tribute* (1988; Bloomsbury)

The Settle-Carlisle Railway (2000; NVM Digital)

Index